Mr Gaanon

SOUTH AMERICA
World Continents Series

● ● ● ● ● ● ● ● ● ● ● ● ● ● ● ● ● ● ● ●

Written by David McAleese and Irene Evagelelis

GRADES 5 - 8
Reading Levels 3 - 4

Classroom Complete Press
P.O. Box 19729
San Diego, CA 92159
Tel: 1-800-663-3609 | Fax: 1-800-663-3608
Email: service@classroomcompletepress.com

www.classroomcompletepress.com

ISBN-13: 978-1-55319-309-8
ISBN-10: 1-55319-309-1

© 2007

Permission to Reproduce

Permission is granted to the individual teacher who purchases one copy of this book to reproduce the student activity material for use in his or her classroom only. Reproduction of these materials for colleagues, an entire school or school system, or for commercial sale is strictly prohibited. No part of this publication may be transmitted in any form or by any means, electronic, mechanical, recording or otherwise without the prior written permission of the publisher. We acknowledge the financial support of the Government of Canada through the Book Publishing Industry Development Program (BPIDP) for our publishing activities. Printed in Canada. All rights reserved.

Critical Thinking Skills

• • • • • • • • • • • • • • • • •

South America

Skills For Critical Thinking	Reading Comprehension				
	Location	Place	Human & Environment Interactions	Movement	Regions
LEVEL 1 Knowledge • Match • Show or Label • List Information • Recall Details (5Ws + H) • Find Information	✓ ✓ ✓ ✓ ✓	✓ ✓ ✓ ✓ ✓	 ✓ ✓ ✓ ✓	✓ ✓ ✓ ✓ ✓	✓ ✓ ✓ ✓
LEVEL 2 Comprehension • Describe & Compare • Summarize • Explain • Select	✓ ✓ ✓ ✓	 ✓ ✓	 ✓ ✓ ✓	 ✓ ✓ ✓	✓ ✓ ✓ ✓
LEVEL 3 Application • Organize Information • Interview • Apply	✓ ✓	✓	✓	✓ ✓ ✓	✓ ✓ ✓
LEVEL 4 Analysis • Conclude • Analyze	✓ ✓	✓ ✓	✓ ✓	✓ ✓	✓ ✓
LEVEL 5 Synthesis • Design • Create					✓ ✓
LEVEL 6 Evaluation • Evaluate • Compare			✓	✓	✓ ✓

Based on Bloom's Taxonomy

Contents

●●●●●●●●●●●●●●●●●

TEACHER GUIDE

STUDENT HANDOUTS

FREE!

✔ **6 BONUS** Activity Pages! Additional worksheets for your students
✔ **12 BONUS** Overhead Transparencies! For use with your projection system

- Go to our website: **www.classroomcompletepress.com/bonus**
- Enter item CC5751 or South America
- Enter pass code CC5751D for Activity Pages. CC5751A for Overheads.

© CLASSROOM COMPLETE PRESS

South America CC5751

Assessment Rubric

• • • • • • • • • • • • • • • •

South America

Student's Name: _____ Assignment: _____ Level: _____

	Level 1	Level 2	Level 3	Level 4
Understanding Concepts	Demonstrates a limited understanding of the concepts. Requires teacher intervention.	Demonstrates a basic understanding of the concepts.	Demonstrates a good understanding of the concepts.	Demonstrates a thorough understanding of the concepts.
Response to the Text	Expresses responses to the text with limited effectiveness, inconsistently supported by proof from the text	Expresses responses to the text with some effectiveness, supported by some proof from the text	Expresses responses to the text with appropriate skills, supported with appropriate proof	Expresses thorough and complete responses to the text, supported by concise and effective proof from the text
Analysis & Application of Concepts	Interprets and applies various concepts in the text with few, unrelated details and incorrect analysis	Interprets and applies various concepts in the text with some detail, but with some inconsistent analysis	Interprets and applies various concepts in the text with appropriate detail and analysis	Effectively interprets and applies various concepts in the text with consistent, clear and effective detail and analysis

STRENGTHS:

WEAKNESSES:

NEXT STEPS:

Teacher Guide

Our resource has been created for ease of use by both TEACHERS and STUDENTS alike.

Introduction

This resource provides ready-to-use information and activities for remedial students in grades five to eight. Written to grade and using simplified language and vocabulary, geography concepts are presented in a way that makes them more accessible to students and easier to understand. Comprised of reading passages, student activities and overhead transparencies, our resource can be used effectively for whole-class, small group and independent work.

How Is Our Resource Organized?

STUDENT HANDOUTS

Reading passages and **activities** (*in the form of reproducible worksheets*) make up the majority of our resource. The reading passages present important grade-appropriate information and concepts related to the topic. Included in each passage are one or more embedded questions that ensure students are actually reading and understanding the content.

For each reading passage there are **BEFORE YOU READ** activities and **AFTER YOU READ** activities. As with the reading passages, the related activities are written using a remedial level of language.

- The BEFORE YOU READ activities prepare students for reading by setting a purpose for reading. They stimulate background knowledge and experience, and guide students to make connections between what they know and what they will learn. Important concepts and vocabulary from the chapters are also presented.

- The AFTER YOU READ activities check students' comprehension of the concepts presented in the reading passage and extend their learning. Students are asked

to give thoughtful consideration of the reading passage through creative and evaluative short-answer questions, research, and extension activities.

The **Assessment Rubric** (*page 4*) is a useful tool for evaluating students' responses to many of the activities in our resource. The **Comprehension Quiz** (*page 31*) can be used for either a follow-up review or assessment at the completion of the unit.

PICTURE CUES

This resource contains three main types of pages, each with a different purpose and use. A **Picture Cue** at the top of each page shows, at a glance, what the page is for.

 Teacher Guide
- Information and tools for the teacher

 Student Handout
- Reproducible worksheets and activities

 Easy Marking™ Answer Key
- Answers for student activities

EASY MARKING™ ANSWER KEY

Marking students' worksheets is fast and easy with this **Answer Key**. Answers are listed in columns – just line up the column with its corresponding worksheet, as shown, and see how every question matches up with its answer!

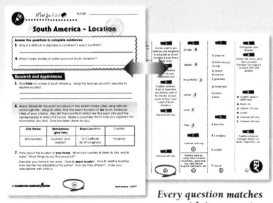

Every question matches up with its answer!

Bloom's Taxonomy

Our resource is an effective tool for any GEOGRAPHY PROGRAM.

Bloom's Taxonomy* for Reading Comprehension

The activities in our resource engage and build the full range of thinking skills that are essential for students' reading comprehension and understanding of important geography concepts. Based on the six levels of thinking in Bloom's Taxonomy, and using language at a remedial level, information and questions are given that challenge students to not only recall what they have read, but move beyond this to understand the text and concepts through higher-order thinking. By using higher-order skills of application, analysis, synthesis and evaluation, students become active readers, drawing more meaning from the text, attaining a greater understanding of concepts, and applying and extending their learning in more sophisticated ways.

Our resource, therefore, is an effective tool for any Geography program. Whether it is used in whole or in part, or adapted to meet individual student needs, our resource provides teachers with essential information and questions to ask, inspiring students' interest, creativity, and promoting meaningful learning.

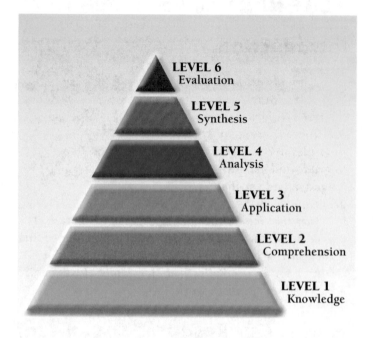

LEVEL 6 Evaluation
LEVEL 5 Synthesis
LEVEL 4 Analysis
LEVEL 3 Application
LEVEL 2 Comprehension
LEVEL 1 Knowledge

BLOOM'S TAXONOMY: 6 LEVELS OF THINKING

Bloom's Taxonomy is a widely used tool by educators for classifying learning objectives, and is based on the work of Benjamin Bloom.

Vocabulary

- hemisphere • sphere • connect • latitude • longitude • links • equator • ancient • civilization • geographer • absolute • exact • relative • location • links • continent • feature • tropical • rainforest • urban • rural • desert • jungles • grasslands • river • route • transportation • languages • humid • dense • export • mountain • unique • physical • characteristics • earthquakes • extinct • wildlife • vegetation • human • environment • interactions • positive • negative • habitats • endangered • species • savannah • products • underground • subway • communication • vehicles • satellite • movement • automobiles • motorcycle • scooter • region • suburbs

South America – Location

1. Read these six geography words to yourself.

continent	hemisphere	geographer	equator	latitude	longitude

Below is a web with the definitions of each of these words. Write the word on the arm of the web that matches its definition. One has been done for you.

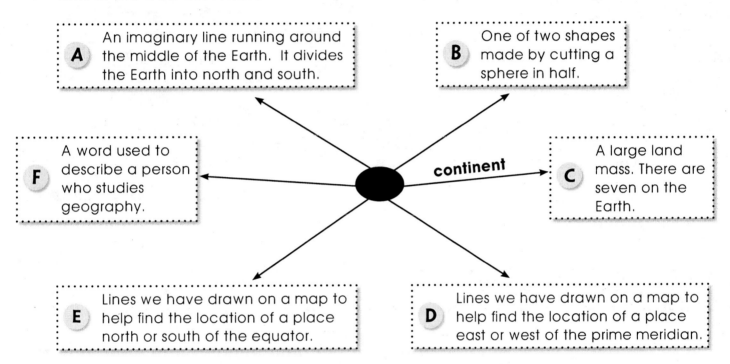

A An imaginary line running around the middle of the Earth. It divides the Earth into north and south.

B One of two shapes made by cutting a sphere in half.

F A word used to describe a person who studies geography.

continent

C A large land mass. There are seven on the Earth.

E Lines we have drawn on a map to help find the location of a place north or south of the equator.

D Lines we have drawn on a map to help find the location of a place east or west of the prime meridian.

2. On the map, color South America in **green**. Show the equator as a **red line**.

NAME: _____

South America – Location

How can we describe the **location** of South America? We can describe its location in two ways. We can describe exactly where it is, or we can describe where it is by using the things we find around it. If we describe exactly where South America is, we are giving its **absolute location**. When we describe the features around South America and the features that connect it to other places, we are describing its **relative location**.

Because South America is one of the world's largest continents, it is very difficult to describe its exact location. Why? We describe absolute location by looking at where lines of **latitude** and **longitude** cross, but because South America is so large, we cannot do this. A **geographer** could say that South America is found approximately between 12°N latitude and 55°S latitude, but those two lines of latitude are more than 5,000 miles apart! From east to west, South America is also about 3,000 miles wide! It is much easier to describe South America's location by looking at those features and places around it.

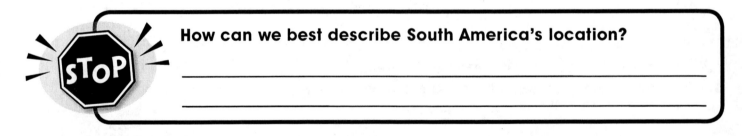

How can we best describe South America's location?

_____

_____

To begin with, South America is entirely in the western hemisphere. Most of South America is also south of the equator. That means that most of it is in the southern hemisphere. Like other continents, it has shorelines on several large bodies of water. The Atlantic Ocean lies to the east, and the Pacific Ocean to the west, and the Caribbean Sea to the north. These bodies of water provide **links** between South America and other parts of the globe. On its northern borders, South America is linked by land to North America at Panama. To the south, across the Drake Passage, South America is only about 600 miles away from Antarctica! By describing these features, we have given South America's relative location.

South America – Location

1. Put a check mark (✓) next to the answer that is most correct.

a) South America is only 600 miles north of which icy continent?

○ **A** North America
○ **B** Asia
○ **C** Antarctica
○ **D** the Arctic

b) From east to west, South America is only about _____ miles wide.

○ **A** 3,000
○ **B** 5,000
○ **C** 600
○ **D** 4,000

c) Most of South America is south of _____.

○ **A** North America
○ **B** Antarctica
○ **C** the equator
○ **D** the Pacific Ocean

2. Circle 🅣 if the statement is true or 🅕 if it is false.

T = True	
F = False	

T   F   a) The Atlantic Ocean lies to the east of South America.

T   F   b) The Pacific Ocean lies to the east of South America.

T   F   c) South America is linked to North America at the equator.

T   F   d) South America is only about 3,000 miles away from Antarctica.

T   F   e) South America is about 3,000 miles wide.

T   F   f) Absolute location tells exactly where a place is.

South America – Location

Answer the questions in complete sentences.

3. Why is it difficult to describe a continent's exact location?

_____

4. Which major bodies of water surround South America?

_____

Research and Applications

5. Find **Chile** on a map of South America. Using the features around it, describe its relative location.

_____

_____

6. Many atlases list the exact locations of the world's major cities using latitude and longitude. Using an atlas, find the exact location of **ten** South American cities of your choice. Also, list the country in which we find each city and the hemisphere(s) in which it is found. Make a chart like this to help you organize the information you find. One has been done for you.

City Name	Hemisphere (give two)	Exact Location	Country
Montevideo	southern and western	34°S latitude 56°W longitude	Uruguay

7. Think about the location of **your home**. What is its number, its street, its city, and its state? What things do you find around it?

Describe your home in two ways. Give its **exact location**. Give its **relative location**. How are the two descriptions the same? How are they different? Share your descriptions with a friend.

NAME: _____

South America - Place

1. Match the word to the illustration that shows it. Match by writing the number from the picture beside the word.

jungle _____

desert _____

 1

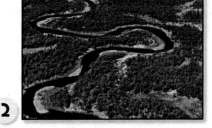 2

mountains _____

urban _____

 3

 4

rural _____

river _____

 5

 6

2. What do you already know about South America? Use the web to show what you know.

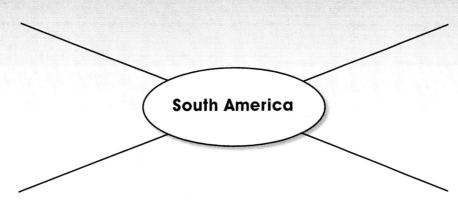

South America

Reading Passage

NAME: _____

South America – Place

How can we describe South America as a place that is different from all other continents? We can look at its unique features. Its **physical characteristics** make it unique. The rainforests, rivers, mountains, and deserts of South America are different from all others. The **people** of South America, where they have chosen to live, and the languages that they speak make it unique. The **wildlife** of South America also makes it different from all other continents. Each of these features helps us better understand South America and describe it as a **place**.

(San Pedro, Chile)

South America has many different physical characteristics. The Andes **Mountains** are both rocky and tree-covered, and stretch high into the sky. The Pampas grassland region is low and covered with wild grasses. The Atacama **Desert** is dry and salty. The Amazon Rainforest is a tropical region with dense, humid **jungles**. This variety of physical characteristics is part of what makes South America unique as a place.

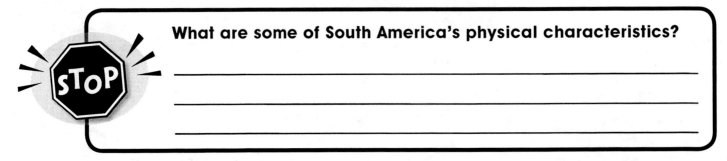

What are some of South America's physical characteristics?

_____

_____

_____

There are huge cities throughout South America, filled with millions of people. Cities like Rio de Janeiro, Sao Paolo, Lima, and Buenos Aires are all major **urban** areas. As on other continents, most of South America's largest cities can be found on major bodies of water, such as the ocean or important **rivers**. Large farms in **rural** areas of Brazil and Argentina provide food for both their people and for **export** to other countries. While many languages are spoken in South America, Spanish and Portuguese are the most common. A variety of aboriginal languages are also spoken.

NAME: _____

South America – Place

1. **Fill in the blank with a word from the list. One word will be left over.**

humid	salty	urban	tropical	grassland
languages	desert	physical	rural	tree-covered

South America is a continent with many _____ characteristics.
                                                                          a

There are tall, _____ mountains called the Andes, a _____
                                  b   c

desert called the Atacama Desert, and _____ rainforests in _____
                                                                  d   e

regions. The Pampas is a large, flat _____. Spanish and Portuguese
                                                                              f

are the two most common _____. Rio de Janeiro is a large,
                                                              g

_____ area. Farms are found in _____ areas.
            h   i

2. Which word matches the definition? Color the arrow that points to the correct word. You may use an atlas or a dictionary to help.

Sao Paolo ⟵	**A** A large city or urban area in South America.	⟶ Pampas
rural ⟵	**B** A word that describes something native to a country.	⟶ aboriginal
desert ⟵	**C** A word that describes an area of dense vegetation, usually one that is very hot and humid, with large amounts of rainfall.	⟶ jungle
export ⟵	**D** A word that describes things that a country sends to other countries for trade.	⟶ import

NAME: _____

South America – Place

Answer each question with a complete sentence.

3. What are the major **languages** spoken in South America?

_____

4. How are the Andes Mountains and the Pampas different?

_____

Research

5. The **Amazon River** is perhaps the most famous river in the world! It is long, wide, and full of many different species of freshwater creatures. Conduct some research on the Amazon River. Use the questions below as a guide. Write two questions of your own that you would like to research. Share your findings with a friend.

a) How long is the Amazon?

b) Which countries does it flow through?

c) Which large body of water does it flow into?

d) How often does the Amazon flood the area around it?

e) My question: _____

f) My question: _____

6. Much of South America was colonized by Spain or Portugal. Because of that, many countries in South America have Spanish or Portuguese as their official languages. Conduct some research to find which countries were colonized by Spain or Portugal, and what their official languages are.

Colonizing Country	New Countries Created by Colonizing Country	Language
Spain	a) b) c)	a) b) c)
Portugal	a) b) c)	a) b) c)

NAME: _____

Human & Environmental Interactions

1. Why are each of the things listed below important to us? How can we help preserve them? List your ideas in the box below each. Share your list with a partner, and then with the class. As you hear other ideas, add them to your list. You may have to remove ideas that do not belong.

a) clean water

b) clean air

c) endangered animals

d) trees

2. What do these words mean? Write each definition. Use a dictionary to help you.

a) environment _____

_____

b) extinct _____

_____

c) rainforest _____

_____

d) earthquake _____

_____

NAME: _____

Human & Environmental Interactions

Every day, the things that people do affect their **environment**. Sometimes people cut down trees for paper or wood for houses, only to destroy the habitats of animals. Sometimes we hunt animals to extinction. Sometimes, the pollution we create affects ourselves and the environment around us. When an environment is harsh or changing, people must often adapt to their environment to survive. Learning about these issues is known as the study of human and environmental **interactions**.

(Amazon River & Rainforest)

Here is an example of a human and environmental interaction that is having a negative affect. In Brazil, the Amazon Rainforest, one of the world's natural wonders, covers most of the northern part of that country. Located along the Amazon River, just south of the equator, this jungle is rich with animal, fish, and insect wildlife. It is also an area in which many kinds of medicines have been discovered by scientists. Much of the air on earth is cleaned by the trees that grow there. However, in spite of these wonderful features, people are cutting down the trees at a very fast pace. The trees are used by people for paper and wood, but when they are cut down many animals lose their natural habitats, and we have fewer trees to clean our air. It is a dangerous situation, and many people are working to find a solution to this problem.

Why is it important to prevent too much of the Amazon Rainforest from being cut down?

_____

_____

Sometimes nature affects the choices we make when deciding where to live and how we build our homes. In Peru, several recent earthquakes have made people think about how they construct their homes and buildings. The worst earthquake happened in 1970, when thousands of people were killed, and their homes were destroyed. Following this disaster, people were more careful about where they built their homes. In recent years, fewer people have died in earthquakes in Peru, because people have learned how to adapt to the danger.

Human & Environmental Interactions

1. **Circle** **T** if the statement is true or **F** if it is false.

		T = True **F = False**

T   F   a) Peru's worst earthquake happened in 1970.

T   F   b) The Amazon Rainforest covers most of northern Brazil.

T   F   c) The trees of the Amazon Rainforest clean much of the Earth's air.

T   F   d) People do not cut down Amazon Rainforest trees.

T   F   e) Because of earthquakes, people in Peru have changed how they build their homes.

2. **Put a check mark (✔) next to the answer that is most correct.**

   a) The Amazon River is just south of _____.
   - ○ **A**   a large city
   - ○ **B**   the Pampas grasslands
   - ○ **C**   the equator
   - ○ **D**   an earthquake in Peru.

   b) Amazon trees that are cut down are used for many purposes, such as _____.
   - ○ **A**   air and water
   - ○ **B**   animals and fish
   - ○ **C**   pollution and habitats
   - ○ **D**   wood and paper

   c) Humans can harm the environment when they _____.
   - ○ **A**   destroy habitats
   - ○ **B**   hunt animals to extinction
   - ○ **C**   cause pollution
   - ○ **D**   all of the above

After You Read 📖

Human & Environmental Interactions

Answer each question with a complete sentence.

3. How must people in an earthquake zone change their way of life?

_____

4. Why is it important for people to find a solution to cutting down too many trees?

_____

Research, Extensions and Applications

5. South America's many regions contain hundreds of different animals, birds, and fish. Using the **Wildlife Organizer** on the next page, find kinds of wildlife unique to each of these areas: the Andes Mountains, the Amazon Rainforest, and the Pampas. Pay special attention to those animals that are **endangered**.

6. What kinds of programs does your school, town, or city have to help protect the environment? Circle one of these areas to research:

| my school | my neighborhood | my town | my city |

Complete a chart like the one below to help you collect your information. Share your chart with the class.

My _____'s Programs	How they help protect the environment

7. What things can you do at home to help protect the environment? List them.

_____

_____

 After You Read

Wildlife Organizer

Use the organizer to record information about the wildlife found in these three famous regions of South America.

Wildlife of the Andes Mountains	Wildlife of the Amazon Rainforest	Wildlife of the Pampas Grasslands
Animal Species:	Animal Species:	Animal Species:
Habitats:	Habitats:	Habitats:
Other Facts:	Other Facts:	Other Facts:

South America – Movement

1. **Think about how you, other people, things, and ideas move from place to place. Beside each example below, write as many different ways as you can think of for moving in that way.**

Going to work ➡ _____

Going to school ➡ _____

Traveling to another country ➡ _____

Traveling to the International Space Station ➡ _____

Delivering new cars ➡ _____

Delivering food to the grocery store ➡ _____

Sharing news ➡ _____

2. **Match the word on the left to its definition on the right. You may use an atlas or a dictionary to help.**

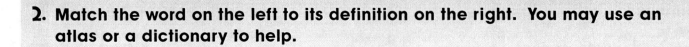

urban	An area outside a city. An example is the country. There are fewer people and services than in a city, and they are spread out across wide areas of land.	A
rural	The sharing of ideas through many different ways, such as through speech, printed words, signals, sign language, and images.	B
transportation	A word describing the area of a town or a city. These areas have a large population, many kinds of transportation, and many services, like police, hospitals and libraries.	C
communication	The word used to describe how humans move themselves and other items from place to place. It includes the vehicles we use and the things they travel on (air, water, roads, etc.).	D

South America - Movement

I n South America, people travel to work, to school, or to recreational activities each day. Their ideas are spread by radios, TV, and newspapers, and by telephone calls, letters, and the Internet. Different kinds of vehicles travel within and between countries delivering the **products** that people and businesses use. Geographers call all of these things **movement**. Movement is a word we use to describe how people, ideas, and products move from place to place.

South America is a continent where people share their ideas in many different ways. Newspapers and radios are very important for sharing ideas. In rural areas, a radio provides a link to larger, urban areas and the world. Ideas are also spread by television or satellite dish, by telephone calls between family and friends, by letters, and by the Internet. Many homes have their own computers and televisions, which allow them to find out what is happening in other parts of the world.

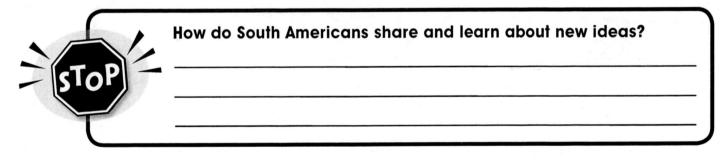

How do South Americans share and learn about new ideas?

_____

_____

_____

Buses, trains, and subways are very important in the crowded **urban** areas of South America. For example, in Buenos Aires, Argentina, and Lima, Peru, thousands of people use buses to get to work or school each day. There are **subways** in some cities to help move people from place to place. Surface trains help bring people from the **suburbs** into the downtown areas.

Throughout South America, people rely on many different forms of **transportation**. Trains help people and products move from place to place, often between **rural** places and cities. Cars, motorcycles, motor scooters, buses, and trucks are also used each day. Some South American cities have large airports, while others have large ports. To travel greater distances, many South Americans fly by plane, or send their products by ship.

After You Read

NAME: _____

South America – Movement

1. Using what you have read in the text, write a definition for each of the following words. Do not use a dictionary to help you. Find the answers in the reading.

a) movement _____

_____

b) transportation _____

_____

c) products _____

_____

d) radio _____

_____

2. Circle T if the statement is true or F if it is false.

T = True	F = False

T F a) Movement is a word that describes how people dance.

T F b) Lima is in Argentina.

T F c) Newspapers are very important for sharing ideas.

T F d) Products are sent by ships or planes over great distances.

T F e) In rural areas, radios provide a link to the outside world.

T F f) There are no computers in South America.

T F g) Many cities in South America are very crowded.

© CLASSROOM COMPLETE PRESS

South America CC5751

South America – Movement

Answer each question with a complete sentence.

3. What are some of South America's most popular forms of transportation? Give an example of how each one is used.

_____

4. How is information spread throughout South America?

_____

Research and Applications

5. Research some of South America's largest cities that have subways. Here are four of them:

Caracas, Venezuela   **Rio de Janeiro, Brazil**
Buenos Aires, Argentina   **Santiago, Chile**

Find information that helps you complete the chart. Share what you've discovered.

City	Country	Number of Subway Lines	Number of Daily Riders	Other Information

6. Think of the city, town, or rural area in which you live. How is movement important to your home? How do transportation routes connect your hometown to other places? Are they connected by roads, by rail, by ship, or by planes? What about how ideas are communicated? Which newspapers, TV programs, or Internet services are available? Create a web like the one below to show the importance of movement to your city, town, or rural area.

```
┌──────────────────────────┐              ┌──────────────────────────┐
│ Communication links in   │              │ Transportation links in  │
│ my city/town/rural area  │              │ my city/town/rural area  │
└──────────────────────────┘              └──────────────────────────┘
                    ┌───────────────┐
                    │  City Name    │
                    └───────────────┘
┌──────────────────────────┐              ┌──────────────────────────┐
│ Communication            │              │ Transportation used      │
│ in my home               │              │ by my family             │
└──────────────────────────┘              └──────────────────────────┘
```

South America - Regions

1. **If you were planning to write a guide book about several rooms in your school, how would you describe each room?**

Think about these things:

     size   **characteristics**   **how and why people use it**

In the box beside each special room's name, give details about that room in your school. Share your **My School's Three Special Rooms** work with a small group of friends.

a) the gym

b) the library

c) _____
    your choice

South America - Regions

A **region** is an area of land that can be either large or small. A region can be described by the **features** that make it **unique**. Things like mountains or a rainforest help make a region unique. These are called **physical characteristics**. A region can also be described by the **languages** that people speak there. **Geographers** are interested in regions because regions can change over time. South America is a continent with many different regions.

(Piranha)

One of the most famous regions in South America, and in the whole world, is the Amazon **Rainforest**. Even though it is found in South America, this rainforest is important to the entire planet. The Amazon Rainforest contains so many trees that it helps clean the air from all over the world. Did you know that scientists search the Amazon Rainforest looking for new medicines to help cure diseases? It is also home to many unique kinds of animals, birds, and fish. Many of these animals are **endangered species**. Unfortunately, the rainforest is threatened by people who cut down its trees without replanting new ones. Thousands of acres of rainforest are lost each month. As these trees are cut down, many animals lose their **habitats**.

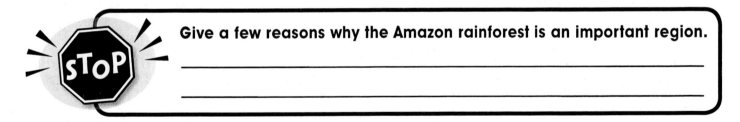

Give a few reasons why the Amazon rainforest is an important region.

_____

_____

Another important region in South America stretches from the northern parts of the continent to the south. This region is called the Andes, a very long and tall **mountain range** that passes through many different countries. The Andes region, especially in Peru, was once the home to the ancient Inca Empire. Many of its ruins can still be found scattered throughout the mountains.

The Pampas is a **grassland** region found on the coast of the Atlantic Ocean in Argentina and Uruguay. Like the **savannahs** of Africa, there are few trees on the Pampas. The summers there are warm and wet, while the winters are cool.

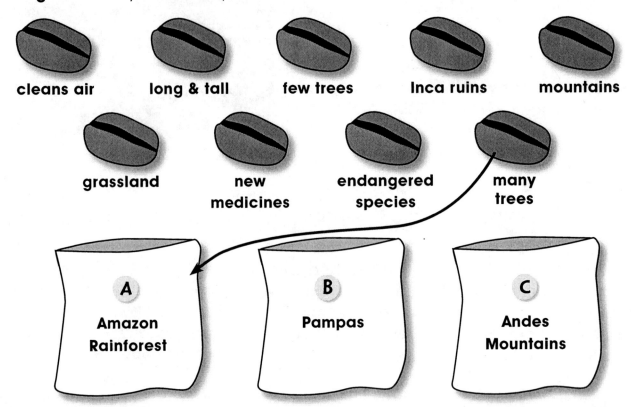

South America - Regions

After You Read

NAME: _____

1. Describe each of these three South American regions by matching features to the correct name. Draw an arrow from the **coffee bean** to the correct **bag** in which you would place it. One has been done for you.

cleans air   long & tall   few trees   Inca ruins   mountains

grassland   new medicines   endangered species   many trees

A Amazon Rainforest

B Pampas

C Andes Mountains

2. **Put a check mark (✔) next to the answer that is most correct.**

a) **The Pampas is a** _____.
○ **A** grassland
○ **B** mountain range
○ **C** river
○ **D** rainforest

b) **When too many trees are cut down, many animals lose their** _____.
○ **A** air
○ **B** water
○ **C** habitat
○ **D** medicine

After You Read

South America - Regions

Answer each question with a complete sentence.

3. Be like a geographer! Describe the Andes Mountains.

_____

4. Which features are used to describe a region?

_____

Research and Extensions

5. Many crops are grown throughout South America. Perhaps the most famous is coffee. Coffee is enjoyed by millions of people around the world each day, but where does it come from? How is it grown? Research coffee, and share your findings with the class. You may wish to present your coffee facts as a display, as a brochure or booklet, or as a Power Point presentation.

Here are some questions to get you started:

- **In which regions of South America is coffee grown?**
- **Where is coffee grown (hills, valleys, etc.)?**
- **What does a coffee plant look like?**
- **What is a coffee bean?**
- **What steps are taken to turn a coffee bean into a cup of coffee?**

6. Some modern countries in South America have been built on the sites of ancient **civilizations**. Thankfully, many ruins and buildings of these ancient civilizations still stand today! This allows us to learn about and appreciate those who lived long ago. Using the **Regions Change Over Time** organizer on the next page, **compare** an ancient South American civilization with the one that exists there now. You will have to conduct some research before filling in the organizer. You may wish to decorate your organizer with drawings or pictures of the things you have discovered during your research (i.e., a drawing of an ancient civilization's ruins compared to a modern city, or a map showing the location of the ancient civilization).

Regions Change Over Time

Ancient Civilization

[ ]

Then

[ ]

[ ]

[ ]

[ ]

[ ]

Modern Name

[ ]

Now

[ ]

[ ]

[ ]

[ ]

[ ]

Name

Location

Movement

Buildings

Language

After You Read 📖

Crossword Puzzle!

equator
medicines
Rainforest
latitude
Panama
Pacific
mountain
absolute
Antarctica
southern
characterisitics
earthquakes
Spanish
hemisphere
geographer

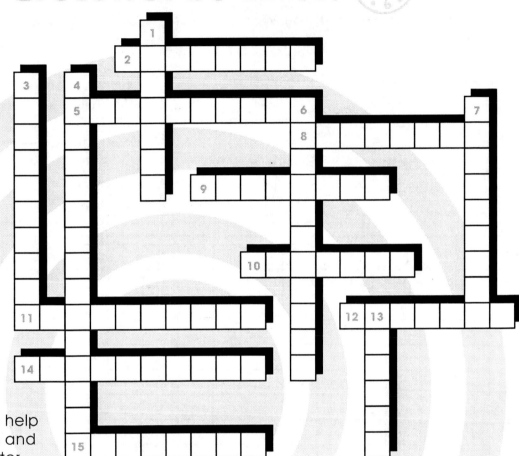

Across

2 Lines on a map to help find a place north and south of the equator

5 One of the shapes made by cutting a sphere in half

8 _____ location describes exactly where a place is.

9 The Andes is a long _____ range in South America.

10 Imaginary line running along the middle of the Earth

11 The Amazon _____ is a region with humid jungles.

12 A common language spoken in South America

14 South America is north of this icy continent.

15 South America is entirely in the _____ hemisphere.

Down

1 The ____ Ocean lies to the west of South America.

3 A person who studies geography

4 A place can be described by physical and human _____.

6 _____ in Peru have changed how and where people build their homes.

7 Scientists look for new _____ in the Amazon Rainforest.

13 South America is linked to North America at _____ .

NAME: _____

Word Search

Find all of the words in the Word Search. Words may be horizontal, vertical, or diagonal. A few may even be backwards! Look carefully!

South America	movement	grassland	latitude
mountains	ideas	aboriginal	urban
Equator	continent	extinct	wildlife
region	interaction	transportation	features
rural	jungle	geographer	environment
languages	links	desert	products
endangered	longitude	rainforest	savannah

u	r	b	a	n	n	o	i	t	c	a	r	e	t	n	i	q	e
s	d	m	o	u	n	t	a	i	n	s	i	j	g	h	j	a	n
x	c	v	d	e	r	e	g	n	a	d	n	e	r	t	u	j	v
s	o	u	t	h	a	m	e	r	i	c	a	a	s	a	t	h	i
q	w	e	r	t	y	u	i	o	p	v	b	b	t	a	r	f	r
t	r	a	n	s	p	o	r	t	a	t	i	o	n	j	a	j	o
s	f	g	h	j	k	f	d	e	s	e	r	t	f	k	i	d	n
f	f	v	m	o	v	e	m	e	n	t	d	a	f	i	n	g	m
s	a	v	a	n	n	a	h	j	k	l	n	m	s	o	f	j	e
f	d	s	a	f	h	t	f	u	u	u	g	h	v	l	o	a	n
y	r	t	y	u	i	u	f	t	d	h	h	c	c	k	r	s	t
d	x	a	s	c	y	r	l	a	t	i	t	u	d	e	e	d	a
q	d	v	n	h	j	e	e	e	e	e	e	l	x	s	f	b	
j	h	g	v	s	d	s	u	b	c	a	d	d	a	t	t	g	o
d	r	t	k	h	j	m	l	o	p	h	f	t	n	i	a	h	r
n	b	n	b	b	h	t	e	s	e	d	f	n	g	n	s	e	i
a	i	d	e	a	s	g	t	m	n	b	g	e	u	c	t	f	g
l	o	n	g	i	t	u	d	e	f	g	n	n	a	t	y	i	i
s	d	f	f	f	y	u	o	i	e	a	o	i	g	v	g	l	n
s	m	g	p	r	o	d	u	c	t	s	i	t	e	e	u	d	a
a	j	u	n	g	l	e	j	u	n	h	g	n	s	r	o	l	l
r	u	r	a	l	t	v	p	i	n	a	e	o	r	t	p	i	d

NAME: _____

Comprehension Quiz

Part A

Circle **T** if the statement is true or **F** if it is false.

T = True
F = False

8

T   F   **a)** Most of South America is north of the equator.

T   F   **b)** The Pacific Ocean is to the west of South America.

T   F   **c)** South America is linked to North America at Panama.

T   F   **d)** The trees of the Amazon Rainforest clean much of the Earth's air.

T   F   **e)** Peru does not have earthquakes.

T   F   **f)** Lima is in Argentina.

T   F   **g)** Latitude and longitude are used to find a place's absolute location.

T   F   **h)** The word **urban** describes an area in a city or town.

Part B

Label the map by doing the following:

6

1. Show the following features on the map by writing the letter on the map in the correct location.

    a) South America
    b) North America
    c) Atlantic Ocean
    d) Pacific Ocean
    e) Caribbean Sea

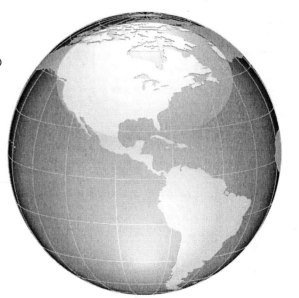

2. Color the equator **red.**

SUBTOTAL: /14

Comprehension Quiz

Part C

Answer the questions in complete sentences.

1. What is the difference between **absolute** location and **relative** location? As an example, describe South America's relative location.   (3)

   _____

   _____

   _____

2. How do we describe **place**? Describe South America as a place.   (3)

   _____

   _____

3. Describe what is meant by **human and environment interactions**. Explain how the cutting down of too many Amazon Rainforest trees is a negative interaction.   (3)

   _____

   _____

4. What do we mean by **movement** in geography? Give one example of transportation and one of communication.   (3)

   _____

   _____

   _____

5. What is a **region**? Describe the Pampas or the Andes Mountains as a region.   (4)

   _____

   _____

   _____

SUBTOTAL: /16

3. Portuguese and Spanish

4. Andes: tall, rocky, and tree-covered
Pampas: low regions covered with wild grasses

5.
a) Length: approx. 4000 miles
b) Brazil, etc.
c) Atlantic Ocean
d) yearly
e) Answers will vary
f) Answers will vary

6. Possible answers:
Portugal: Brazil, etc.
Spain: Argentina, etc.

EZ✓

1.
a) physical
b) tree-covered
c) salty
d) humid
e) tropical
f) grassland
g) languages
h) urban
i) rural

2.
A Sao Polo
B Aboriginal
C Jungle
D export

1.
jungle **4**
desert **6**
mountains **1**
urban **3**
rural **5**
river **2**

2. Answers will vary

Possible answers:
rocky, tree-covered mountains, grasslands, dry, salty deserts, tropical rainforests, etc.

3. It is too vast to use latitude and longitude to pinpoint an exact location where these lines cross

4. Atlantic Ocean, Pacific Ocean, Caribbean Sea

5. Possible answers: West of Argentina and Bolivia; east of the Pacific Ocean, south of Peru; west coast of South America

6. Answers will vary

7. Answers will vary

Using relative location because the continent is so vast

1.
a) Ⓑ C
b) Ⓑ A
c) Ⓑ C

2.
a) T
b) F
c) F
d) F
e) T
f) T

1.
A equator
B hemisphere
C continent
D longitude
E latitude
F geographer

2.

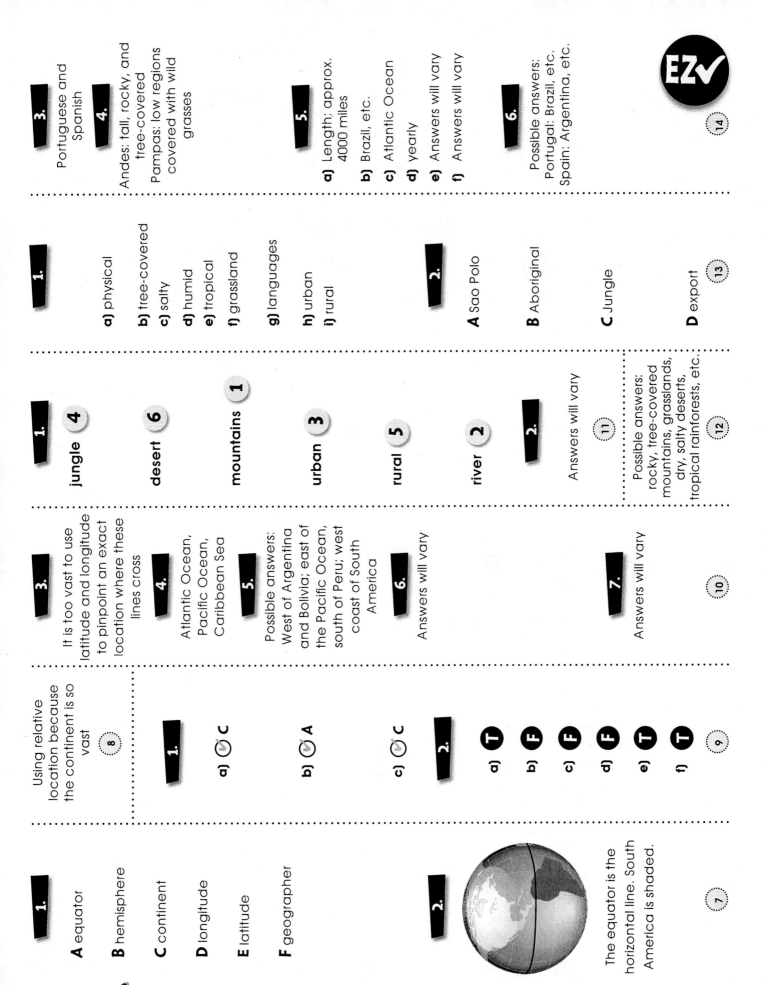

The equator is the horizontal line. South America is shaded.

© CLASSROOM COMPLETE PRESS

EZ✓

1. Possible answers:
a) how people, ideas, and products move from place to place.
b) vehicles and the routes on which they travel.
c) the things we buy and use in our homes.
d) a device for communicating ideas, music, etc.

2.
a) F
b) F
c) T
d) T
e) T
f) F
g) T

(22)

Possible answers: radio, Internet, TV, etc.

(21)

1. Answers will vary

2.
A rural
B communication
C urban
D transportation

(20)

3. Possible answer: Change the way they build their homes

4. Possible answer: Destroys trees needed for cleaning the air and animal habitats

5. Answers will vary in detail depending on resource used. Some possibilities: Andes – llama, alpaca, etc. Amazon rainforest – monkeys, leopard, etc. Pampas – farm animals, cattle, etc.

6. Answers will vary

7. Answers will vary

(18)

1.
a) T
b) T
c) T
d) F
e) T

2.
a) C
b) D
c) D

(17)

1. Possible answers:
a) drinking, cooking, etc.
b) breathing, etc
c) not many left, protect, etc
d) oxygen, reforestation, etc.

2. Possible answers:
a) all that surrounds us (living things, climate, air, water, and land)
b) no longer existing as a species
c) a jungle with a high amount of rainfall
d) the shaking of the land when the energy is released at a fault in the earth's crust

(15)

Possible answers: The Amazon rainforest helps clean much of the earth's air, and many species live there.

(16)

Across:

2. latitude
5. hemisphere
8. absolute
9. mountain
10. equator
11. Rainforest
12. Spanish
14. Antarctica
15. southern

Down:

1. Pacific
3. geographer
4. characteristics
6. earthquakes
7. medicines
13. Panama

3. Tall, long, both rocky and tree-covered, etc.

4. Geographers look at physical characteristics, languages spoken, and where and how people live.

5. Answers will vary depending upon choices and resources used. Possibilities: Columbia, hills, a bush, etc.

6. Answers will vary

1.

A Cleans air, new medicines, endangered species, many trees

B Few trees, grassland

C Long and tall, Inca ruins, mountains

2.
a) A
b) C

Possible answers: Medicines are discovered there, endangered species, trees clean our air, etc.

1. Answers will vary

3. Possible answers: Train, subway, car, bicycle, motor scooter

4. Possible answers: Radio, Internet, TV, etc.

5. Answers will vary in complexity and detail depending on the resources used. (i.e. Rio de Janeiro – 2 subway lines, buses are more popular)

6. Answers will vary

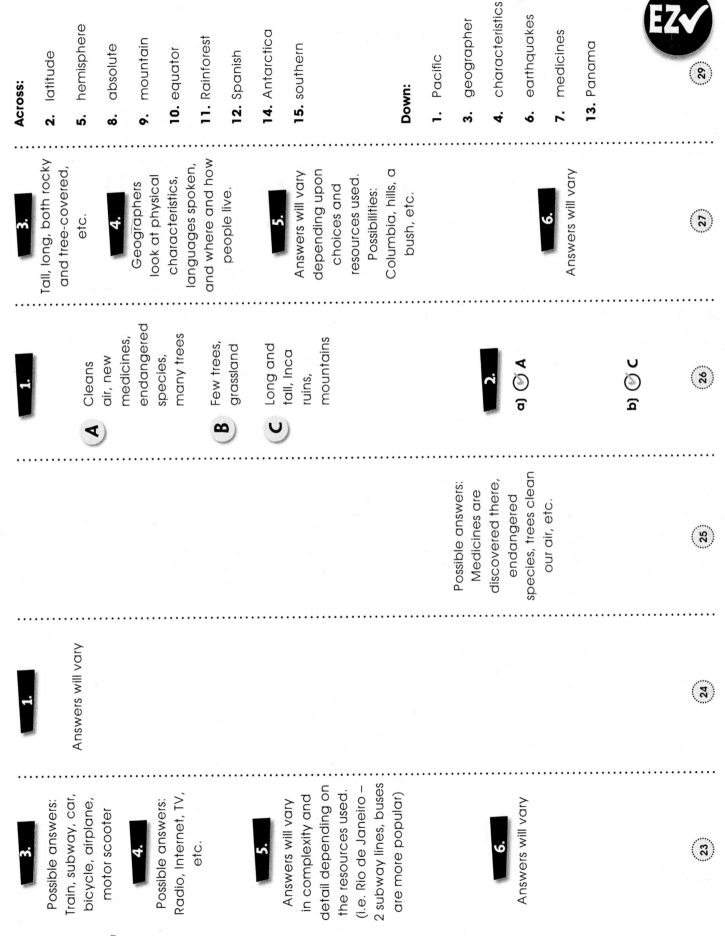

23 24 25 26 27 29

EZ✓

EZ✓

Word Search Answers

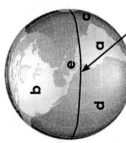

Part A

a) **F**
b) **T**
c) **T**
d) **T**
e) **F**
f) **F**
g) **T**

h) **T**

Part B

equator

Part C

1. Possible answers:
Absolute location – a place's exact location using latitude and longitude
Relative location – described by the features around it, and the connections it has to other places
South America – south of North America and the Caribbean, east of the Pacific Ocean, west of the Pacific Ocean

2. Possible answers:
Mountains, grasslands, deserts, towns, cities

3. Possible answers:
How humans and the environment interact, in both positive and negative ways;
Cutting down trees – loss of habitats, fewer trees to clean the air

4. Possible answers:
How people, ideas, and products are moved from place to place (i.e. train, plane, car, ship, bus, bicycle, e-mail, radio, television, Internet, telephone)

5. Possible answers:
Large or small area of land described by:
Physical characteristics, vegetation, language
Pampas – flat, low grasslands, wild grasses
Andes – tall, long, both rocky

30

31

32

South America
World Location Map

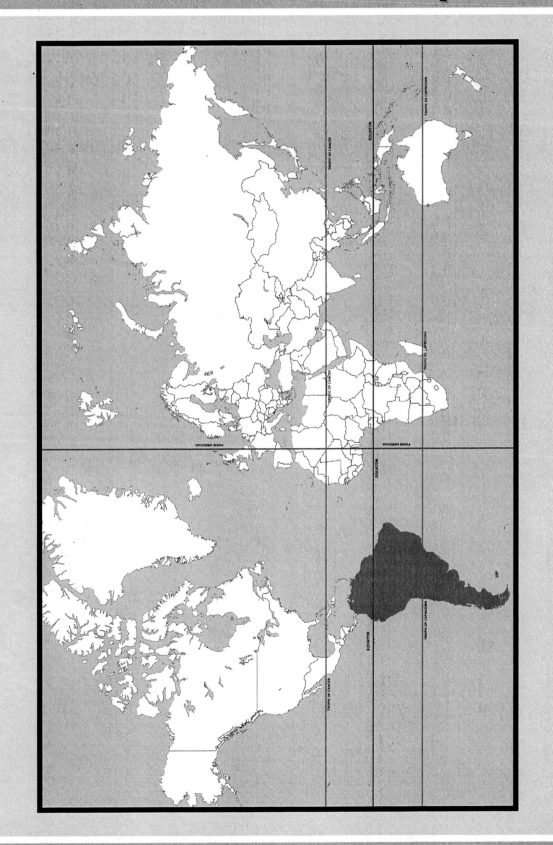

© CLASSROOM COMPLETE PRESS

South America
Globe View Map

South America
Outline Map

EQUATOR

TROPIC OF CAPRICORN

El Salvador
Nicaragua
St Vincent & the Grenadines
Grenada
Barbados
Panama
Venezuela
Trinidad & Tobago
Costa Rica
Colombia
Suriname French Guiana
Guyana
Ecuador
Peru
Brazil
Bolivia
Paraguay
Chile
Argentina
Uruguay
Falkland Islands
South Georgia
Tierra Del Fuego

© CLASSROOM COMPLETE PRESS

South America
Physical Map

Guatemala
El Salvador   Nicaragua
Costa Rica   Panama
Venezuela
St Vincent & the Grenadines   St Lucia
Grenada   Barbados
Trinidad & Tobago
Colombia
Suriname   French Guiana
Guyana
Ecuador
Peru
B r a z i l
Bolivia
Pacific Ocean
Paraguay
Chile
Argentina
Uruguay

```
0          750        1,500 Miles

0      750    1,500 KM
```

Falkland Islands

South Georgia

Tierra Del Fuego

© CLASSROOM COMPLETE PRESS

South America CC5751

South America
Major Population Map

Country
★ **National Capitals**
● Major City

© CLASSROOM COMPLETE PRESS

South America
Political Map

© CLASSROOM COMPLETE PRESS

South America Transportation Map

Belize
Jamaica
Haiti
Dom. Rep.
Rico
St Kitts & Nevis
Antigua & Barbuda
Cape Verde
Honduras
Caribbean Sea
Dominica
Guatemala
El Salvador
Nicaragua
St Vincent & the Grenadines
St Lucia
Barbados
Grenada
Panama
Costa Rica
Venezuela
Trinidad & Tobago
Colombia
Suriname
French Guiana
Guyana
Ecuador
Peru
B r a z i l
Bolivia
Paraguay
Chile
South Pacific Ocean
Argentina
Uruguay

Road Ways
—— Primary Roads
━━ Highways

0	750	1,500 Miles
0	750	1,500 KM

Falkland Islands
South Georgia
Tierra Del Fuego

© CLASSROOM COMPLETE PRESS

South America CC5751

South America
Waterway Map

Waterways

Major Lakes

Major Rivers

South Pacific Ocean

0   750   1,500 Miles

0   750   1,500 KM

Guatemala
El Salvador   Nicaragua
Costa Rica   Panama

Caribbean Sea

St Vincent & the Grenadines
Grenada
St Lucia
Barbados

Venezuela

Trinidad & Tobago

Colombia

Surinam   French

Guyana

Ecuador

Amazon   Negro

Peru

Jurua   Purus   Madeira   Amazon

Juruena

Xingu

Iriri

B r a z i l

Itenes

Bolivia

Paraguay

Chile

Salado

Uruguai

Argentina

Uruguay

Falkland Islands

South Georgia

Tierra Del Fuego

© CLASSROOM COMPLETE PRESS

South America
Continent Outline Map

© CLASSROOM COMPLETE PRESS

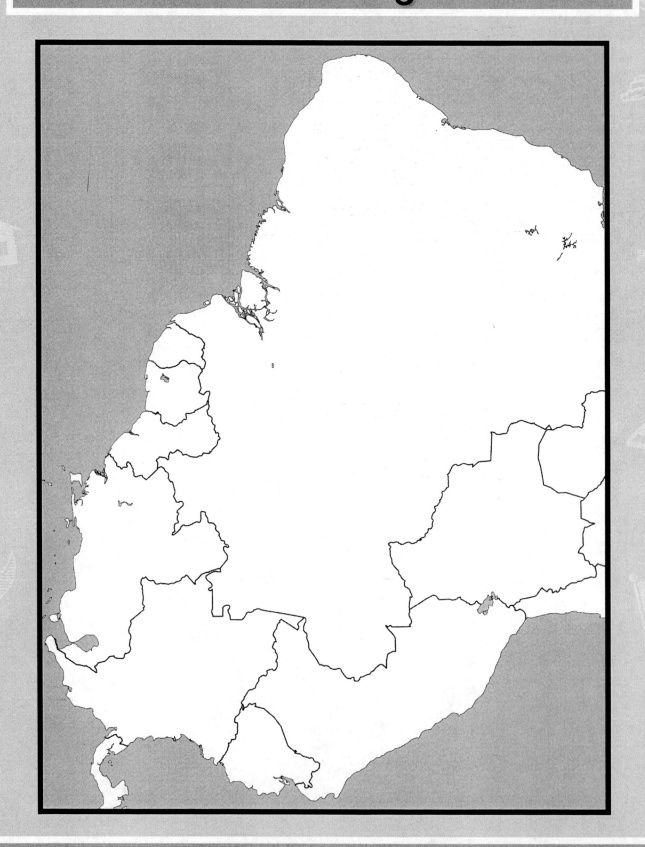

© CLASSROOM COMPLETE PRESS

South America CC5751

South America
Southern Region

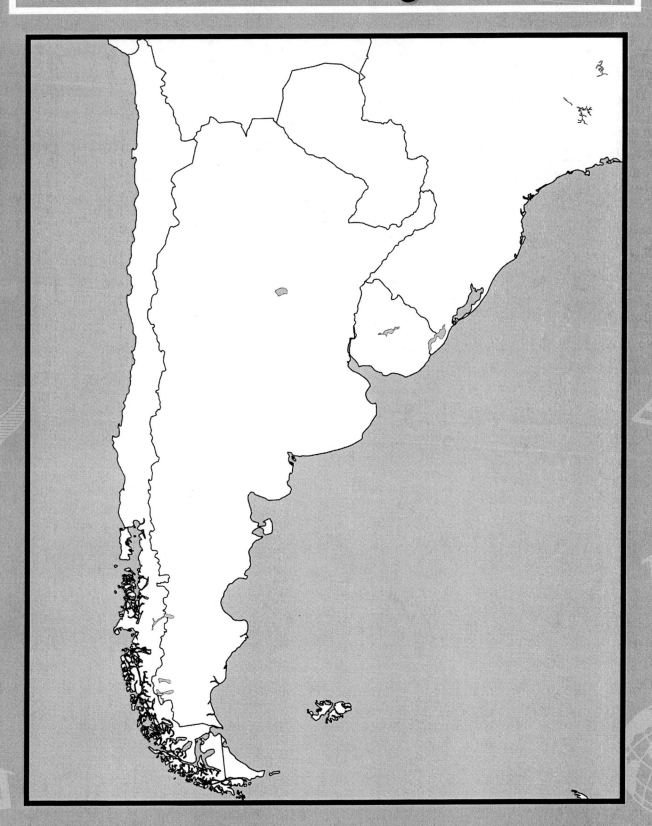

© CLASSROOM COMPLETE PRESS

South America CC5751

South America
Caribbean Region

© CLASSROOM COMPLETE PRESS

South America
Outline Map

© CLASSROOM COMPLETE PRESS

© CLASSROOM COMPLETE PRESS

Publication Listing

•••••••••••••••••••

Ask Your Dealer About Our Complete Line

REGULAR EDUCATION
••••••••••••••••••

REMEDIAL EDUCATION
Reading Level 3-4 Grades 5-8
••••••••••••••••••

LANGUAGE ARTS

ITEM #	TITLE
	LITERACY SKILL SERIES
CC1106	Reading Response Forms: Grades 1-2 NEW!
CC1107	Reading Response Forms Grades 3-4 NEW!
CC1108	Reading Response Forms Grades 5-6 NEW!
CC1109	Reading Response Forms Big Book NEW!
CC1110	Word Families - Short Vowels: Grades K-1 NEW!
CC1111	Word Families - Long Vowels: Grades K-1 NEW!
CC1112	Word Families Big Book: Grades K-1 NEW!
	LITERATURE KITS GRADES 1-2
CC2100	Curious George (H. A. Rey)
CC2101	Paper Bag Princess (Robert N. Munsch)
CC2102	Stone Soup (Marcia Brown)
CC2103	The Very Hungry Caterpillar (Eric Carle)
CC2104	Where the Wild Things Are (Maurice Sendak)
	LITERATURE KITS GRADES 3-4
CC2300	Babe: The Gallant Pig (Dick King-Smith)
CC2301	Because of Winn-Dixie (Kate DiCamillo)
CC2302	The Tale of Despereaux (Kate DiCamillo)
CC2303	James and the Giant Peach (Roald Dahl)
CC2304	Ramona Quimby, Age 8 (Beverly Cleary)
CC2305	The Mouse and the Motorcycle (Beverly Cleary)
CC2306	Charlotte's Web (E.B. White) NEW!
CC2307	Owls in the Family (Farley Mowat) NEW!
	LITERATURE KITS GRADES 5-6
CC2500	Black Beauty (Anna Sewell)
CC2501	Bridge to Terabithia (Katherine Paterson)
CC2502	Bud, Not Buddy (Christopher Paul Curtis)
CC2503	The Egypt Game (Zilpha Keatley Snyder)
CC2504	The Great Gilly Hopkins (Katherine Paterson)
CC2505	Holes (Louis Sachar)
CC2506	Number the Stars (Lois Lowry)
CC2507	The Sign of the Beaver (E.G. Speare)
CC2508	The Whipping Boy (Sid Fleischman)
CC2509	Island of the Blue Dolphins (Scott O'Dell) NEW!
CC2510	Underground to Canada (Barbara Smucker) NEW!
CC2511	Loser (Jerry Spinelli) NEW!
	LITERATURE KITS GRADES 7-8
CC2700	Cheaper by the Dozen (Frank B. Gilbreth) NEW!
CC2701	The Miracle Worker (William Gibson) NEW!
CC2702	The Red Pony (John Steinbeck) NEW!
CC2703	Treasure Island (Robert Louis Stevenson) NEW!
CC2704	Romeo and Juliet (William Shakespeare) NEW!

ENVIRONMENTAL STUDIES

ITEM #	TITLE
	MANAGING OUR WASTE SERIES
CC5764	Waste: At the Source
CC5765	Prevention, Recycling & Conservation
CC5766	Waste: The Global View
CC5767	Waste Management Big Book
	CLIMATE CHANGE SERIES
CC5769	Global Warming: Causes NEW!
CC5770	Global Warming: Effects NEW!
CC5771	Global Warming: Reduction NEW!
CC5772	Global Warming Big Book NEW!

SOCIAL STUDIES

ITEM #	TITLE
	WORLD CONTINENTS SERIES
CC5750	North America
CC5751	South America
CC5768	The Americas Big Book
CC5752	Europe
CC5753	Africa
CC5754	Asia
CC5755	Australia
CC5756	Antarctica
	NORTH AMERICAN GOVERNMENT SERIES
CC5757	American Government
CC5758	Canadian Government
CC5759	Mexican Government
CC5760	Governments of North America Big Book
	WORLD GOVERNMENT SERIES
CC5761	World Political Leaders
CC5762	World Electoral Processes NEW!
CC5763	Capitalism versus Communism NEW!
CC5777	World Politics Big Book NEW!
	WORLD CONFLICT SERIES
CC5500	American Civil War
CC5501	World War I
CC5502	World War II
CC5503	World Wars I & II Big Book
CC5505	Korean War NEW!
CC5506	Vietnam War NEW!
CC5507	Korean & Vietnam Wars Big Book NEW!

SCIENCE

ITEM #	TITLE
	ECOLOGY & THE ENVIRONMENT SERIES
CC4500	Ecosystems
CC4501	Classification & Adaptation
CC4502	Cells
CC4503	Ecology & The Environment Big Book
	MATTER & ENERGY SERIES
CC4504	Properties of Matter
CC4505	Atoms, Molecules & Elements
CC4506	Energy
CC4507	The Nature of Matter Big Book
	HUMAN BODY SERIES
CC4516	Cells, Skeletal & Muscular Systems
CC4517	Nervous, Senses & Respiratory Systems
CC4518	Circulatory, Digestive Excretory & Reproductive
CC4519	Human Body Big Book
	FORCE & MOTION SERIES
CC4508	Force
CC4509	Motion
CC4510	Simple Machines
CC4511	Force, Motion & Simple Machines Big Book
	SPACE & BEYOND SERIES
CC4512	Space - Solar Systems
CC4513	Space - Galaxies & The Universe
CC4514	Space - Travel & Technology
CC4515	Space Big Book

VISIT:

www.CLASSROOM COMPLETE PRESS.com

To view sample pages from each book